Sounds Are HIGH
Sounds Are LOW

Sounds Are HIGH
Sounds Are LOW

By Lawrence F. Lowery

Illustrated by Betty Fraser

NSTA Kids
National Science Teachers Association

National Science Teachers Association

Claire Reinburg, Director
Wendy Rubin, Managing Editor
Andrew Cooke, Senior Editor
Amanda O'Brien, Associate Editor
Amy America, Book Acquisitions Coordinator

ART AND DESIGN
Will Thomas Jr., Director
Joseph Butera, Cover, Interior Design
Original illustrations by Betty Fraser

PRINTING AND PRODUCTION
Catherine Lorrain, Director

NATIONAL SCIENCE TEACHERS ASSOCIATION
David L. Evans, Executive Director
David Beacom, Publisher

1840 Wilson Blvd., Arlington, VA 22201
www.nsta.org/store
For customer service inquiries, please call 800-277-5300.

Lexile® measure: 420L

NSTA is committed to publishing material that promotes the best in inquiry-based science education. However, conditions of actual use may vary, and the safety procedures and practices described in this book are intended to serve only as a guide. Additional precautionary measures may be required. NSTA and the authors do not warrant or represent that the procedures and practices in this book meet any safety code or standard of federal, state, or local regulations. NSTA and the authors disclaim any liability for personal injury or damage to property arising out of or relating to the use of this book, including any of the recommendations, instructions, or materials contained therein.

Library of Congress Cataloging-in-Publication Data

Lowery, Lawrence F., author.
  Sounds are high, sounds are low / Lawrence F. Lowery ; illustrated by Betty Fraser.
     pages cm -- (I wonder why)
  Audience: K to 3.
  ISBN 978-1-941316-04-7 -- ISBN 978-1-941316-98-6 (e-book)
  1. Sound--Juvenile literature. I. Fraser, Betty, illustrator. II. Title.
  QC225.5.L68 2014
  534--dc23
                        2014019382

Cataloging-in-Publication Data are also available from the Library of Congress for the e-book.

Introduction

The *I Wonder Why* series is a set of science books created specifically for young learners who are in their first years of school. The content for each book was chosen to be appropriate for youngsters who are beginning to construct knowledge of the world around them. These youngsters ask questions. They want to know about things. They are more curious than they will be when they are a decade older. Research shows that science is students' favorite subject when they enter school for the first time.

Science is both *what* we know and *how* we come to know it. What we know is the content knowledge that accumulates over time as scientists continue to explore the universe in which we live. How we come to know science is the set of thinking and reasoning processes we use to get answers to the questions and inquiries in which we are engaged.

Scientists learn by observing, comparing, and organizing the objects and ideas they are investigating. Children learn the same way. The thinking processes are among several inquiry behaviors that enable us to find out about our world and how it works. Observing, comparing, and organizing are fundamental to the more advanced thinking processes of relating, experimenting, and inferring.

The five books in this set of the *I Wonder Why* series focus on some content of the physical sciences. The physical sciences consist of studies of the physical properties and interactions of energy and inanimate objects as opposed to the study of the characteristics of living things.

Physics, along with mathematics and chemistry, is one of the fundamental sciences because the other sciences, such as botany and zoology, deal with systems that seem to obey the laws of physics. The physical laws of matter, energy, and the fundamental forces of nature govern the interactions between particles and physical entities such as subatomic particles and planets.

These books introduce the reader to several basic physical science ideas: exploration of the properties of some objects (*Rubber vs. Glass*), interaction with the properties of light and the effect of light on objects (*Light and Color; Dark as a Shadow*), the nature of waves and sound (*Sounds Are High, Sounds Are Low*), and the use of simple machines to accomplish work (*Michael's Racing Machine*).

The information in these books leads the characters and the reader to discover how opaque objects block light and cast shadows, that different objects have special and useful properties (glass and rubber), that simple mechanical tools reveal some of the laws of physics, and that "nontouchable items" such as light and sound energy also have distinctive properties.

Each book uses a different approach to take the reader through simple scientific information. One book is expository, providing factual information. Several are narratives that allow a story involving properties of objects and laws of physics to unfold. Another uses poetry to engage the characters in hands-on experiences. The combination of different styles of artwork, different literary ways to present information, and directly observable scientific phenomena brings the content to the reader through several instructional avenues.

In addition, the content in these books supports the criteria set forth by the *Common Core State Standards*. Unlike didactic presentations of knowledge, the content is woven into each book so that its presence is subtle but powerful.

The science activities in the Parent/Teacher Handbook section in each book enable learners to carry out their own investigations related to the content of the book. The materials needed for these activities are easily obtained, and the activities have been tested with youngsters to be sure they are age appropriate.

After completing a science activity, rereading or referring back to the book and talking about connections with the activity can be a deepening experience that stabilizes the learning as a long-term memory.

Sounds are high.

Sounds are low.

What high sounds do you know?

Is the ring or ding of a bell a high sound?

What can a cow do?

Mooooooooooooooooooo!

When a cow makes a sound,
it is a low sound.

What other things make low sounds?

Animals make different sounds.
Some animal sounds are high.
Some animal sounds are low.

What are some animal sounds
that you know?

Sounds can be loud, high or low.

What high loud sounds do you know?

Have you heard a sound go *CLANG CLANG CLANG*?

Sounds can be loud, high or low.

What low loud sounds do you know?

Do you know anything that goes *CLING CLING CLING*?

Sounds can be soft, high or low.

What high soft sounds do you know?

Have you heard rainfall go *tap tap tap*?

Sounds can be soft, high or low.

What low soft sounds do you know?

Do you know anything that makes low soft sounds?

Sounds can be imagined, high or low.

In a make-believe story about mice,
you can imagine sounds that are nice.

You can imagine a sound that goes *snip snip snip*.

You can imagine a sound that goes *snap snap snap*.

What things do you know that go *snip snip snip*?

What things do you know that go *snap snap snap*?

Have you ever heard anything go *snip snap snip*?

Sounds can be music, high or low.

What sounds of music do you know?

Some sounds of music go *plink plink plink.*

Some sounds of music go *plunk plunk plunk.*

Have you ever heard a sound go *plinkety plink plunk*?

Sounds can be noisy, high or low.

What makes noisy sounds?

Do you know?

Sometimes we think very loud sounds are noisy sounds.

Have you ever heard a loud sound go *BIM BOOM BAM*?

Sounds can be quiet, high or low.

What quiet sounds do you know?

Have you ever heard a sound go *swish swish swish*?

Sometimes sounds go *swish*.

Sometimes sounds go *shhhh*.

Do you know anything that goes *swish swish shhhh*?

Some sounds are strange, high or low.
Are there any strange sounds that you know?

Have you ever heard a sound go *whoooo whoooo whoooo*?

Some strange sounds go *hoooo*.
Some strange sounds go *hooot*.

Do you know of anything
that makes these sounds?

Most people like certain sounds,
high or low.

What sounds do you like?
High or low?
Loud or soft?

Sounds that we like are sounds we call nice.

You may want to hear them once,
you may want to hear them twice.

What sounds do you like to hear over and over again?

Sounds we do not like are unpleasant sounds.
What ones do you know?

Are these unpleasant sounds?
Boom! Crash! Bang! Clunk! Crack! Crash!

You can hear sounds go *pop pop pop*.

What things make popping sounds?

There are high and low sounds in your imagination.
There are high and low sounds in real life.

Some are soft, some are loud, some are like a noisy crowd.
Some are very nice to hear, like music coming to your ear.

Parent/Teacher Handbook

Introduction

This book was written for children who are just beginning to learn how to read. It presents some fundamental concepts related to sounds—pitch and volume. The vocabulary and sentence structure of this book were designed so the book can be read aloud to a youngster. The semi-poetic structure, the repetitive rhythm of the words, and the reuse of consonant sounds in single-syllable words make the content easy to follow and remember.

Because this is a book on sounds, the sounds of words when they are spoken is part of the content. In addition, the science content is the recognition that some sounds are high and some are low (a property of sound called pitch), and some are loud and some are soft (a property called volume). This book attempts to sensitize the young reader to the tremendous variety of vibrating objects that produce sounds.

The questions, written in verse form, challenge readers to think about sounds they experience, and the illustrations invite further conversations about sounds.

Inquiry Processes

Hearing is one of the ways we observe the world in which we live. *Sounds Are High, Sounds Are Low* provides the reader with practice in observing with their ears. The sense of hearing is an important phase of observing that is sometimes overlooked in science-related activities.

Our five senses serve us well to take in information and learn about the world around us. We see, taste, feel, smell, and hear. Through experiences and practice, those avenues into our brains build our knowledge. Because the story in this book focuses on the sense of hearing, it invites the young beginning reader to think about sounds and provides some practice in hearing and listening. With additional activities, we can all become better listeners and we will learn more about the world in which we live.

Content

The story line of this book focuses only on the sensory (hearing) properties of sound. The properties of pitch and volume serve as a base for understanding a more abstract property of sound—that sounds are always made by something in vibration. The activity section of this book builds on the story line by suggesting simple activities that introduce the idea that sounds—pitch and volume—are made by vibrations.

Vibrations create waves, and the number of vibrations (waves) per second is called the frequency of sound. The human ear is most sensitive to a frequency of about 3,000 vibrations per second. The hum of a motor, the sound made by human vocal cords, and the sounds from strings of a musical instrument all originate in one common source: vibrating objects. The chart on the next page provides some information on the range of vibrations that can be heard.

Scientists explain that the pitch of a sound is determined by the frequency of its vibrations. The low frequency or low pitch of the cow's *moo* and the high pitch or high frequency of the telephone ring can be easily differentiated by the average human ear.

Research on learning suggests that pitch and volume are easily understood by young children and vibrations are a more complex and abstract concept that is better understood after learning about pitch and volume at the hearing-experience level. Thus, the content for the text is not about vibration. It is about pitch and volume because these characteristics of sound serve as a basis for understanding vibrations.

The activities in the next section build on pitch and volume by providing a simple beginning set of experiences that introduce the concept of sound vibrations.

Science Activities

Comparing Sounds at Different Times of the Day

Keep a list of the different sources of sounds you hear at a particular location during a 15-minute period of the day. Report about the sounds that you heard. Do this again at night in the same location. How do the day sounds compare with the night sounds?

Hearing Variations in Pitch

There are several experiences in which a youngster can hear differences in high and low sounds.

1. Run a fingernail over the fibers of a cloth-covered book or stroke a pencil or stick across the teeth of a comb, wood file, or corrugated cardboard. The youngster can note that the faster the movement, the higher the sound.

2. An adult can use a hand saw to cut through a board. The child can note that the faster the teeth cut across the board, the higher the sound.

3. Hold a playing card against a turning bicycle wheel and note the change in the sound as the wheel speeds up or slows down.

Pitch Scale

Frequency: Vibrations Per Second (VPS)	Examples		
About 16	Lower limit of human hearing		
20–200	Deep bass tones (27 VPS = lowest note on the piano)		
256	"do"	Middle C	
278		C - sharp	
294	"re"	D	
312		D - sharp	
330	"mi"	E	
349	"fa"	F	
370		F - sharp	"Middle" Musical Scale
392	"sol"	G	
416		G - sharp	
440	"la"	A	
466		A - sharp	
494	"ti"	B	
512	"do"	C	
525–3,000	Normal adult conversation		
4,000	About the highest tone used in music		
8,000	High pitched, shrill tones		
About 20,000	Upper limit of human hearing		
About 30,000	Upper limit of hearing for dogs and cats		
About 100,000	Upper limit of hearing for bats		

Hearing Variations in Volume

Produce a sound by tapping a drinking glass or bottle with a pencil, plucking a one-string instrument, or blowing a whistle. Make the sound again by putting more effort into the tap, pluck, or blow. Repeat using less effort. After describing differences in each sound, the youngster will realize that because the object produces only one note, the difference must be caused primarily by the effort put into its production (loud sounds require more effort than soft sounds.)

Additional activities can be found at www.nsta.org/sounds.